THERE'S A TRICERATOPS IN THE TREE HOUSE

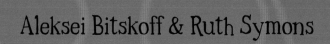

Aleksei Bitskoff & Ruth Symons

QED Publishing

Triceratops was a **big** plant-eating dinosaur with three

Design: Duck Egg Blue
Managing Editor: Victoria Garrard
Design Manager: Anna Lubecka
Dinosaur Expert: Chris Jarvis

First published in the UK in 2013 by
QED Publishing
A Quarto Group company
230 City Road
London EC1V 2TT

www.qed-publishing.co.uk

A catalogue record for this book is available from the British Library.

ISBN 978 1 78171 482 9

Printed in China

massive horns on his head!

He lived around

70 million

years ago – many millions of years before the first humans appeared.

But just imagine if Triceratops was alive today! How would he cope with modern life?

What if Triceratops joined a football team?

He had sturdy legs for racing up and down the pitch.

But he might **POP** the ball with his sharp horns!

With his metre-long horn the size of a hockey
stick, Triceratops would be great at ice hockey.

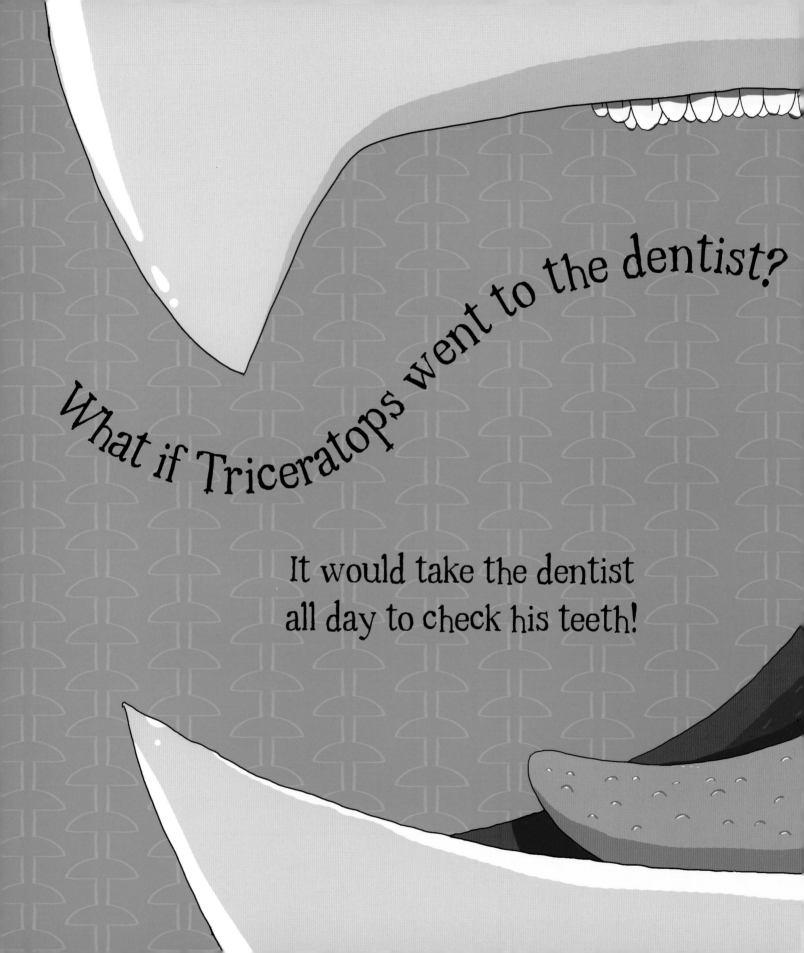

What if Triceratops went to the dentist?

It would take the dentist
all day to check his teeth!

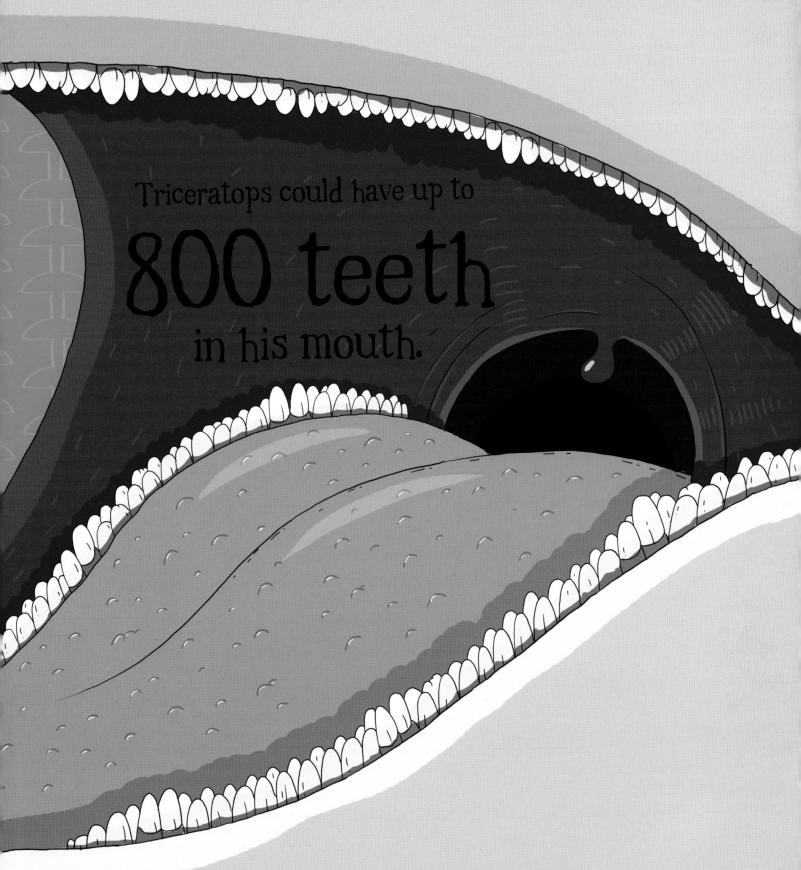

Triceratops could have up to

800 teeth

in his mouth.

What if Triceratops caught the train?

At 9 metres long, Triceratops was almost
the size of a train carriage.

He wouldn't fit in with the other passengers.

But he could travel in the
goods wagon!

What if Triceratops went on holiday?

With his sharp, parrot-like beak, Triceratops could easily crack open coconuts. They would make a tasty drink for everyone on the beach!

But Triceratops would rather munch on palm leaves. His sharp teeth were perfect for slicing them up.

Was Triceratops taller than my dad?

Triceratops was much **taller** than any human. His skull alone was taller than your dad – it was 2.5 metres long!

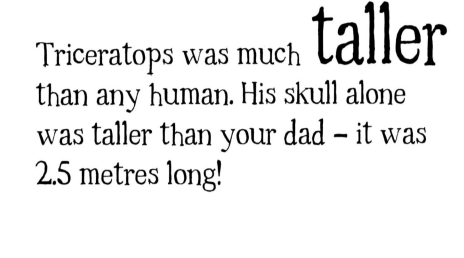

Baby Triceratops was much smaller than its parents. Its head was only just bigger than yours!

What if Triceratops went on a school trip?

He would have great fun – especially at a castle. He could pretend to fight like a knight!

Triceratops wouldn't need armour, as his **thick skin** was good protection.

He wouldn't need a lance because he had **two long horns** on his head.

And he was **bigger** than any horse!

What if Triceratops took a ride in a hot air balloon?

It would have to be a very BIG balloon!

Triceratops weighed 4.5 tonnes.
That's as much as 200 children!

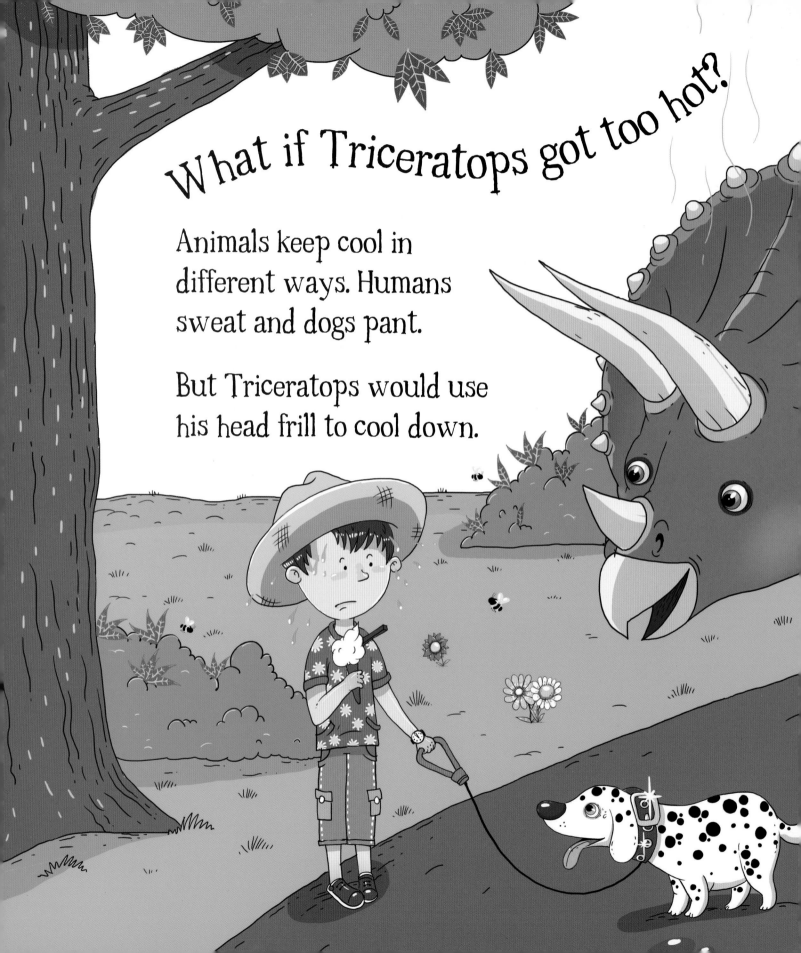

What if Triceratops got too hot?

Animals keep cool in different ways. Humans sweat and dogs pant.

But Triceratops would use his head frill to cool down.

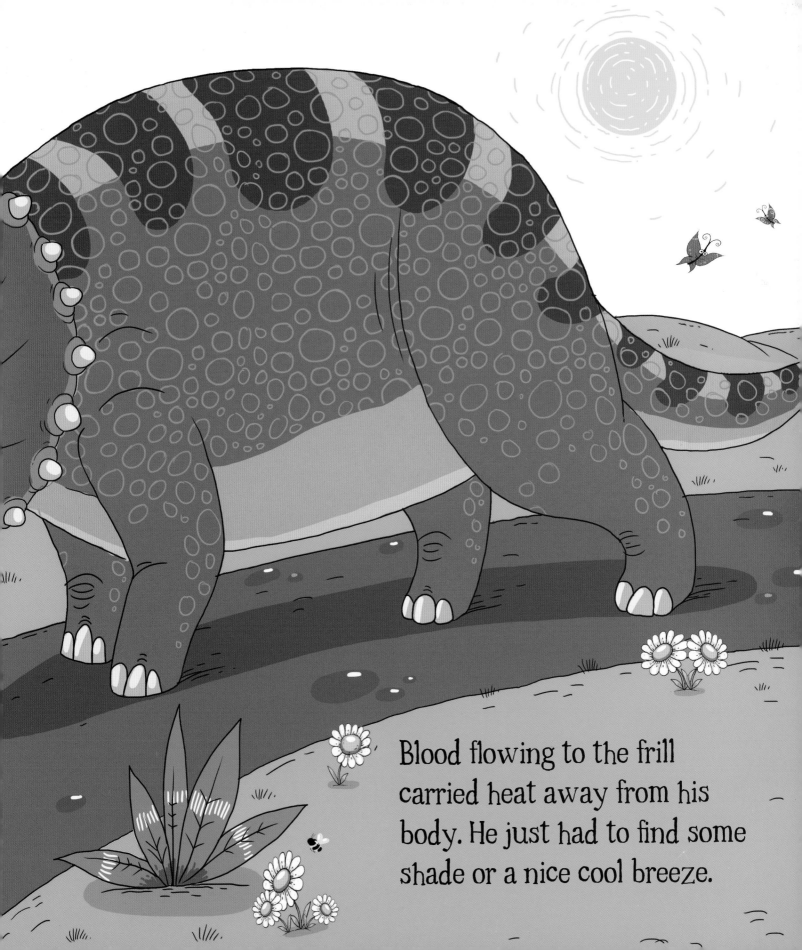

Blood flowing to the frill carried heat away from his body. He just had to find some shade or a nice cool breeze.

What if Triceratops came to my tree house?

He'd be too **big** and **heavy** to get in the tree.

And his thick legs and chunky feet would make it hard to climb the ladder.

But he'd help you all get down!

Triceratops's skeleton

Everything we know about Triceratops comes from fossils – skeletons that have been in the ground for thousands and thousands of years.

Scientists can look at fossils to work out how dinosaurs lived in the past.

This means we know lots about dinosaurs, even though no one has ever seen one!

X-RAY 1192289775982-

MODEL No.: nx110005306 195714613344

big heavy tail

thick sturd legs

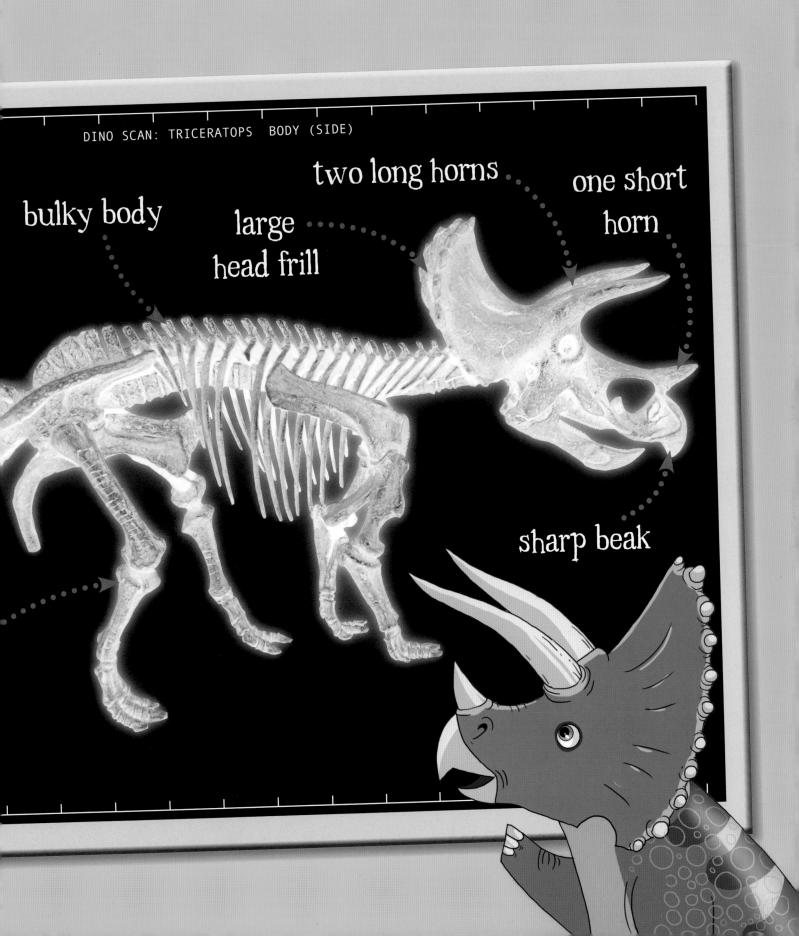

DINO SCAN: TRICERATOPS BODY (SIDE)

two long horns

one short horn

bulky body

large head frill

sharp beak

PASSPORT

Triceratops

(TRY-SAIR-A-TOPS)

NAME MEANS 'THREE-HORNED FACE'

WEIGHT 4.5 TONNES

LENGTH 9 METRES

HEIGHT 3 METRES

HABITAT SCRUBLAND, BUSH, PRAIRIES

DIET FERNS, PALM LEAVES, OTHER PLANTS

T<TRI<<TRICERATOPS<<<<<<<<<<<<632107254374523<<<<<<<<<<<<<<<<0032622976542501>>>>>>>>>